P is for Poetry

by

Julie Fox

authorHOUSE®

AuthorHouse™
1663 Liberty Drive
Bloomington, IN 47403
www.authorhouse.com
Phone: 1-800-839-8640

First published by AuthorHouse 5/12/2010

ISBN: 978-1-4520-1372-5 (sc)

Library of Congress Control Number: 2010905333

Printed in the United States of America
Bloomington, Indiana

This book is printed on acid-free paper.

This book is dedicated to

My family, friends, and students new and old!

May all your dreams come true!

P is for

Penguins
Pigs
And Panda Bears
Pumpkins
Peaches
And juicy pears,
Play-dough
Puzzles
Painting too,
Popcorn
Pickles
Peter Who?
P is for
Pigeon
Party
And potpourri,
Best of all
P is for Poetry!

Blue Dragon

There once was a blue dragon
Who blew blue smoke,
I tell the truth
This is no joke!

Until one day a bare bear came,
And promised to change
The color of his flame.

All he asked was for some hair
So he didn't have to continue
To wear
fancy poka-dotted underwear.

All worked out in the end
And believe it or not
They each made a new friend!

Sometimes

Sometimes
I am as strong as a lion
Those days
I'm not crying,

Other days I am
as clever as a fox
And convince my sister
to play in the box,

There are days when
I am as sweet as a bunny,
I snuggle
and call my mama honey.

Some days
I am as wild as a bear
Brave, strong
and without fear!

At times
I am as silly as a goose
I dance around
and shake my caboose!

There are days
I am as quiet as a mouse,
I tip toe
around the house!

Put them all together
and you get me!
Me, Me, Me
Oh yes sir-ree!

Bamboozle

Tricky, Tricky Ricky
That is his name
Playing tricks
Is his game…

Bamboozle!
Bam-what?
Don't you see the 5 foot walnut?

Bamboozle!
Bam-who?
Is that a green mouse on your shoe?

Bamboozle!
Bam-how?
Do you see the chocolate cow?

Bamboozle!
Bam-when?
Did you see the dancing hen?

Tricky, Tricky Ricky
That is his name
Playing tricks
Is his game!

Words are like Magic

"Do you know any magic words?"
Asked the beautiful squawking birds.

"Listen closely,
pull up a chair
You are going to learn
some magic here!"

"Instead of saying
I *love* that color blue,
You could say
I *adore* that magical hue."

If you want to say,
"Oops, you made a *mistake* on that wall."
You could say,
"Oops, you made a *snafu*, but very small."

When you want to say,
"I am feeling very *hungry* right now!"
You could say,
"My, I am so *famished* I could eat a cow."

If you are going to have
a fun *party* and invite me,
Be sure to invite
your friends to your *jubilee*!

Getting the idea? It is as easy as pie!
Now it is your turn to give it a try!

Clouds

White pony, white pony,
On a tiny hill,
When the wind stops,
You all stand still.
When the wind blows,
You gallop away slow.
White pony, white pony,
Where will you go?

Cupcakes and Brownies

Cupcakes and brownies
with milk to drink,
That's the number one supper,
I surely think;
When I'm all grown
and can have what I please,
I think I will always
insist upon these.

What would you choose,
when you're offered a treat?
When your parents ask
what would you like best to eat?
Is it ice cream with chocolate,
or peanut butter and marshmallow toast?
It's milk with cupcakes
and brownies that I love most!

Mouse and The Moose

Way up North where there's winter snow,
A mouse stepped on a moose's toe.
The moose said, with tears in his eyes,
'Pick on somebody your own size.'

Seven Wonders of the World

I wonder why
The snow is white,
I wonder why
There are stars at night.

I wonder why
The sky is blue,
I wonder why
We say ah-choo.

I wonder why
The grass is green,
I wonder why
Monsters are mean.

I wonder if it is time to go,
maybe I can play in the snow?

School Lunch

I've eaten dirt
and I've eaten flies,
I've eaten frog's spawn
and moldy French-fries,

But nothing is quiet as gross,
As the school's lunch
Broccoli, spinach, and avocado on toast!

Autumn
Brisk, Colorful
Raking, jumping, carving
Pumpkins in the windows
Fall

Millions of Mice

It all started with just two
Living in a cobblers shoe,
Soon there were four
Then quickly six more!

Now there were ten
And one lovely Rhode Island hen….

It didn't take long for 1,000 mice
Some name *Mo, Curly* and *Bryce*
Then there were 1,000 more
Trying to play Nintendo 64

The numbers grew quickly each day
The Rhode Island Hen ran away.
The numbers grew by day and night
There were thousands more by daylight

Until one day there were 1,000,000 mice
And the cobbler said,
"Well, isn't this nice!"

Mr. Fussy Pants

Mom calls me 'Mr. fussy pants'
because most days
I'd rather eat red ants.
I refuse to eat peas,
I find broccoli make me queasy
And carrots make me sneeze.
We fight like mad at meal times,
But I always seem to win
'Cause Mom knows I'll eat anything
If it comes in a box, can or tin!

October

October is a royal queen,
In dress of scarlet and gold.
She dances around the meadows,
When nights are crisp and cold.
The maples flame with bright bouquet,
Which were once a hue of green.
Fuzzy milkweeds, purple asters, and goldenrod
Bow low to greet their queen.

Teddy Bear

Dear Teddy,

You make me feel joyful when I am sad
You put giggles in my heart when I am feeling mad

You always listen to what I have to say
You are always agreeable when we play!

Your heart is like candy,
so very sweet
But you're much better than that sugary treat

I will love you forever,
till the very end
Teddy Bear, Teddy Bear
You are my very best friend!

Love,

Me

Do you Believe?

One night before bed
I saw a little elf.

He had a coat of red
And a little green hat
When he saw me peeking
He quickly sat.

I approached him slowly
And I brought him a treat,
He began to giggle
And jumped to his feet.

He began to dance
His silly little jig,
Then he whispered
"You're mighty big"

We both began to laugh
And fell to the floor.
I thought to myself,
No one will believe what I saw!

Christmas Eve

Late Christmas Eve
When all are asleep,
Appears Christmas mouse
Without a peep!

He means no harm
Just sharing the joy,
Feeling the excitement
From every girl and every boy.

Blinking lights
So colorful and bright,
Just like a carnival
On a warm summer night.

Sugarplums, candy canes, and cookies too,
Treats in big stockings
What is a mouse to do?

He's not greedy
Just a nibble here and there,
He's very thankful
You've learned how to share!

There is Something in my Nose!

There is something
In my nose,
I surely hope it's not
My brother's stinky toes!

If it's a spider
I think I'll scream,
If it's a cockroach
I hope it's a dream.

If it's a feather
It will certainly tickle,
If it's a chicken bone
I am in a pickle!

If it's a tuna
I'll weep right now,
If it's a crab
I'll have a cow!

Maybe it's just a hornet stinger
Oh My!
It's just my pointer finger!

Make Way for Pizza

Start with the dough,
Round and round it will go,
Add some sauce
And a cup of cheese too,
And whatever pleases you.
Ham, pepperoni, olives galore,
You can even add much more!
Make way for pizza,
That's cooked just right
Hurry up and take a bite!

Pizzazz

Allure
Appeal
Dazzle,
Flair
Moxie
Oomph,
Zeal
Zest
Zing
Zip, zip, zip!

In a Small, Small House!

In a small, small house
Lived a small, small mouse.
He liked to dance on the pantry floor,
And peek around the kitchen door.
He nibbled on the cheese and bread,
But preferred tacos instead.
And after dinner he liked his tea,
And often shared it with Mr. Bee.
And after tea
He liked a mint,
Then off to bed he quickly went.
Right to bed without a peep
Mr. Mouse fell fast asleep!

Penelope Mc Flea

I am Penelope Mc Flea
I own a sandwich store
Yummy and delicious
You haven't seen this many sandwiches before
100 choices
Too hard to resist
Do yourself a favor
Try some sandwiches on my list;
Donut dumpling pickles on rye,
Eel marmalade with a side of fly,
Liver pineapple pie with tuna milkshake,
Ketchup, relish, and squid pancake,
Sauerkraut, chicken lard on wheat,
Pickled octopus with frog's feet,
Cheese and brussel spout smores,
Yogurt , onions with a side of apple core.
Marmalade oysters with honeydew,
Fudge mayonnaise sardine stew,
I am Penelope McFlea,
I own a sandwich store
Plenty of unique choices
At Sandwiches Galore!

Cloudy with a Chance of Gumball

It all started one day
As normal as could be,
When I felt a raindrop
Fall down on me.
But soon the raindrops
Were green, red, and blue,
Really tiny ones and large ones too.
Children were cheering
And dancing around
As each gumdrop
Hit the ground.
This weather was awesome
Quiet a delight,
It rained gumdrops
'Till late that night.
Then things got fuzzy
As I saw a light beam
Suddenly I realized
It was just a dream!

If You Give a Frog a Fly

If you give a frog a fly,
Then he'll ask you for bumble-bee on rye.
If you give him bumble-bee on rye,
He'll ask you for a mosquito pie.
If you give him a mosquito pie,
He'll ask you for a party or he'll cry.
If you give him a party
He'll ask you to invite his best friend Marty,
Then he'll ask if Marty can stay
Until next Saturday.
He'll say they will laugh, frolic, and play
He will tell you they won't cry,
Until it is time to say good-bye.
And when they have to say good-bye
Little frog will ask you for a fly!

Emma and Bill

Emma and Bill
Climbed up a hill,
To see what they could see.
Once on top
They decided to stop,
And take a look around.
They looked left and right,
And saw and amazing sight.
They looked up and down,
And spotted tracks on the ground.
They were new and clear,
They were from a baby bear!
Now Emma and Bill
Loved animals so,
But they knew it
Was time to go!

Little Snowflake

Little Snowflake
Falling from the sky
Twirling and dancing
From way up high!
Down you come
One by one and
Two by two,
Everyone is watching you.
With beauty and grace
Down you fall
Turning the forest
Into a winter ball!

Red

Red is like the sound of a cardinal
in the early morning.
Red is the smell of a rose blowing in the wind.
Red is like the taste of a cherry popsicle
fresh from the freezer.
Red is like the feel of a soft blanket.
by Calvin Fox

Friendship

Friendship makes you smile
Like a warm summer day.
Friendship blossoms
Like a flower in May.
Friendship brings you joy
Like a brand new birthday toy.
Friendship is a unique treasure
That only time will measure!

Mr. Monkey

I woke up this morning
with a monkey on my back,
I don't know where he came from
but he was on the attack!
He pulled my left ear
then my right,
I told him to stop it
so we started to fight!
It didn't last long
because he broke into song,
He told me he loved me
I was the apple of his eye,
He was just feeling hungry
could I bake him a pie?

There's a Giraffe on my Bus

There is a giraffe on my bus
and no one seems to care,
Even the bus driver has a weird, strange, stare.
I look to the left
and what do I see?
A howler monkey looking at me!
I peek to the right
and what do I find?
A large lizard of some kind!
Oh my, what's a kid to do?
What's this?
I just heard someone MOO!
Was it Timmy or Tommy
or possibly Sue?
I think my bus is heading to the zoo!

Have You Ever?

Have you ever met a shark,
that thought he was an talking aardvark?
Have you ever met a pig,
who wore a curly, red wig?
Have you ever met a goat,
who pranced around in a leather coat?
Have you ever met a fish,
who promised to grant you a secret wish?
Have you ever met a wallaroo,
who was the manager of a zoo?
Me either!

Butterflies

Shorter days and cooler air,
We all know
The time is near.
The milkweed will go,
And so must we,
To join the rest
Of our family.
We will use our wings
That are bold and bright,
To take us on a
Long, long flight.

On The Farm

Horses, goats, cows that moo

Chickens, bunnies, piglets too

Fish and ducks swim in the lake

Don't forget the garden snake!

All these animals you can see

If you go to the farm with me!

Blessings

My sweet children lets show our love,
by counting our blessings from above.
A milky moon in the night sky,
Twinkling stars way up high;
Green grass with a touch of due,
Dancing flowers in every hue;
Birds that live in the big oak tree
Fish that swim in the deep blue sea;
Roots and shoots that grow real tall,
Fruits and vegetables that feed us all;
Falling raindrops and the warm toasty sun,
That make playing with friends lots of fun.
Blessings here and blessings there
Blessings can be found everywhere!
Count your blessings 1, 2, 3
Let's not forget you and me!

Ladybug

Lady bug wears
A red and black spotted cape.
When it opens up
And changes shape -

Now two wings lift her
straight into the air.
I wish I had
Such a pretty cape to wear!

My Little Ant

I have a little ant,
And I'm very fond of him;
He climbs on to my shoulder,
And then up to my chin;
He crawls down my arm,
And then down my leg;
Now he's a tired little ant
So I tuck him into bed.

A Witch's Broom

I borrowed a witch's broom

and rode far above the town;

I saw the place where the sun comes up

and the place where the moon goes down.

I had an adventure, one of a kind,

inside a great big cave.

and after I tended to the bats,

I rode above a tidal wave.

I visited torrid lands

and mighty jungle ways,

places from long ago

and hints of future days.

You can borrow the broom too

and cross the desert sands,

search for pirate gold

in faraway lands.

How?

Read a book!

Apple of my eye

I found the apple of my eye
While scrounging around for some left over pie,
She was dazzling with beauty
She was quiet a cutie.
She was reaching for cheese
When she whispered,
"Will you help me please?"
I just stared with delight
At this beautiful sight.
I slid across the floor
Toward the mouse I most adored.
I tipped my hat
And then spotted a Tom cat.
I yelled,
"See you later,
Alligator!"

Crocodile Tears

Crocodile Kyle
Why won't you smile?
What seems to make you blue?
Is it Gary Goat
Or Springhorn Sandy
Lizard Linny
Or Is it Rhino Randy
who brings those tears?
Maybe it's
Harry Hunter that you fear!

Doctor's Office

My doctor said
I need a shot
I simply said,
I do not!
Don't worry
It won't hurt a bit,
There's no reason to throw a fit.
Count to three
And we'll be done,
And you'll be ready for fun, fun, fun!
Oh no, that won't do,
Time to fling my
Brother's shoe!
Now I dash for the door,
As I slide across the doctor's floor.
Here comes mommy and doctor too
Oh my goodness, they have super glue!

Missing!

Mr. Cottontail is getting ready

For that most important day

Coloring eggs, making baskets

Easter is on its way!

Everyone was busy

And had a job to do

Rita Raccoon, Maurice the Mole

Even squirrel Sue,

That's when someone sent

A secret note to me

It stated Mr. Cottontail is missing

Oh where ever could he be?

Mr. Cottontail must be found

We shall look all around

We must find him

And set him free

Oh please won't you help me?

Georgie Porgie

Georgie Porgie and Silly Sue
Lived in a giant porcelain shoe,
Georgie Porgie planted beans
And
Silly Sue kept everything tidy and clean.
They had no money
This was true,
But it didn't
make them blue.
They often giggled
and laughed out loud,
this would bring
a curious crowd.
Soon enough they would
buy his beans,
then they had more money
then anyone had ever seen!

Tickled Pink

I knew a girl
Who was tickled pink,
It happened quick,
In just one blink.
It wasn't from a painting brush,
Or even from too much blush,
She wasn't tickled by a flea,
She was just happy to see me!

I'm not a Turkey

I'm not a turkey

Can't you see?

I'm simply an old wallaby

Tasty food, I am not,

I will make your liver rot.

So keep moving right along

Your hunting instincts are all wrong!

I'm not a turkey

Can't you see?

I am simply an old wallaby!

TOFURKEY

Tofurkey is a silly word

I think you will agree,

It rhymes with

Honeybee

Fruit tree

And flea too,

Just to name a silly few.

I think I could continue

To name more words that rhyme,

But I'm very certain

We would simply run out of time.

So I, myself, will stop right here

But you may continue....

If you **DARE!**

Pet Peeves

I have several pet peeves
I would like to share,
Number one
Folding my brother's underwear.
Pet peeve number two
Gum on my shoe.
Pet peeve three and four
When I am sleeping on the floor,
And Uncle Wes begins to snore!
Pet peeve number six,
When my dad eats the last Twix.
Pet peeve seven and eight
When Cousin Kelly brings her date,
And he decides to eat off my plate.
Pet peeve number nine
Being last in line.
Last but not least,
Pet peeve number ten,
When the blue ink runs
Out of my pen!

Purple Hippo

There was a purple hippo
Learning how to ski,
He looked kinda clumsy
As he zoomed by me.
He tilted to the left
And he tilted to the right,
Then tumbled down the mountain
Until he was out of sight.
We raced down the mountain
Me, Madison, Brooke and Jan,
But there was no more hippo
Just a clumsy snowman!

Wolf's Story

Have you heard the story
About the wolf named Willy?
He was not very strong
Just very silly.
He danced a jig
With the three little pigs,
He sang a song
When little red came along,
He stood on his head
And jumped on his bed.
He did a twist and a shout
And flipped all about,
He flipped in a ditch
And needed a stitch
And that is Wolf Willy.

Platypus Paints

Platypus Paints

Each day and night

Always creating a beautiful sight.

A blob of red

And a blob of blue,

Will create a purple hue.

A little yellow

And a little red,

Will create a color

Perfect for a pumpkin's head.

A stroke of yellow

And a stroke of blue,

Will create something new.

Such as grass, trees or a beautiful fern

Now grab a paintbrush

It is your turn.

Doo-Doo MaGoo!

One Monday Morning
I walked into school,
Feeling great, so very cool.
Until Megan gave a shout,
Sniffing and smelling with her sensitive snout.
Something reeks an awful smell,
What is that stench she began to yell!
It smells like a farm, it smells like a zoo
I think that smell is coming from you!
Oh my, oh my I think it's true
I have Doo-Doo MaGoo
on the bottom of my shoe!

I'm in a Pickle

I am in a pickle
It is true
I would never
Lie to you!

It all started when grandma came,
She brought me a gift
For of my new found fame.

I was chosen for the lead part,
My teacher told me
It was only for the very smart.

The play was called
A *Pickle's Life,*
You guessed it
I'm the pickle and I have a wife!

Grandma brought me a pickle suit,
She told me I look mighty cute!
Oh My, I 'm in a pickle!

I Blew a Bubble

I blew a big bubble
Yes it's true
I think it was the
Size of you!

I chewed and chewed
And chewed some more,
I bought it at
The corner store.

That's when Lou
Gave me the dare,
He said I couldn't do it
And I still sleep with a teddy bear!

I showed Lou
What I could do,
I blew a bubble
And it grew and grew.

Lou stopped and began to stare
That's when it popped
All in his hair!

Then Lou began to cry
He grabbed his teddy bear
And yelled "Good-bye!"

Extra Activities

P is for poetry

- Reread with a friend and practice fluency.
- Pick a letter of the alphabet and create your own poem.
- Can you think of any other words that start with P?
- Play the letter sound game. With a friend(s) have one person start by saying a word that starts with the letter *a*. Then the next person has to quickly say a word that starts with *b*. Continue the game until you go through the alphabet.

Blue Dragon

- Find all the homophones in the poem
- Create your own story using homophones
- Sort the words in the story into different categories
- Think about a time you made a new friend. Write a story about it.

Sometimes

- Can you make any text to self, text to text, text to world connections?
- Write some similes about yourself.
- Write a simile poem about an animal.

Bamboozle, Words are like Magic, and Pizzazz

- Look in the dictionary and discovery 3 new vocabulary words. Then try to write a poem about them.
- Think about a time you played a trick on someone. Write a story about it.
- Read the poem with a friend.
- Find words you use often and find synonyms for them.
- Create your own synonym concentration game using index cards.

Clouds

- Change the poem using an animal you love.
- Go outside and look at the clouds. Keep a journal of all the objects and animals you see.
- Study the different kinds of clouds.
- Write a story about where you think the ponies go.

Cupcakes and Brownies and Make Way for Pizza

- What is your favorite supper? Why?
- Use your senses and describe your favorite food.
- Interview your friends and create a graph of your favorite foods.
- What is your favorite pizza topping?
- Write the steps down on how to make your own pizza.

Mouse and the Mouse

- Practice the poem for fluency.
- Think about a time when you felt picked on. How did it make you feel?
- What advice would you give to someone who is being picked on?
- Create a commercial why it is important to be nice to others.

Seven Wonders of the World

- Write a story/poem about things you wonder about.
- If you could change the color of the grass what color would you make it? Why?
- Illustrate a story for this poem.

School Lunch

- What is your favorite school lunch? Describe it.
- Pretend you have been asked to create a new menu for your school's lunch program. What types of foods would you serve?
- Take a survey of your school's top lunch.

Autumn

- Describe your favorite season.
- What type of things do you like to do in the fall/autumn?
- Take a class survey which is the most popular season.
- How many words can you come up with that can describe autumn.
- How many friends or relatives have their birthday in autumn?

Millions of Mice

- How many ways can you make 100?
- Describe how you feel about mice?
- What would you do with a million mice?
- How can you make one million?

Mr. Fussy Pants

- Do you like peas? Your answer is your opinion. Make up a list of your opinions. Then ask your friends if they agree with you. Then make up a list of facts, things that are true. Copy all your opinions and facts on index cards. Then you can play a concentration game.
- You could also play fact or opinion with your cards. You play like the card game war or red or black.

October

- Practice the poem for fluency.
- Who is a royal queen?
- What does she do?
- Create a poem with your own metaphors.

Teddy Bear

- Write a letter to someone special to you.
- Who puts giggles in your heart? Make them a card.
- What do you like to do when you feel sad?
- What is your favorite stuffed animal?
- Have a teddy bear day.

Do you Believe?

- What would you do if you saw an elf?
- Who would you tell if you saw an elf?
- Have you ever saw something that you thought no one else would believe you?
- Draw a picture of something you would like to see.

Christmas Eve

- What do you think happens in your house when you are asleep?
- Go back through the poem and highlight all the words that rhyme.
- Think about a time you had to share. Write a poem about it.

There is something in my Nose!

- Reread the poem for fluency with a friend.
- Write your own poem titled: *There is something in my Ear!*
- Highlight all the rhyming words.

In a Small, Small House

- Can you make a text to text connections?
- Write down the mouse's steps in order.
- What do you like to do when you are at home?

Penelope Mc Flea

- If you have wheat bread and white bread, turkey, ham, and roast beef, how many sandwich combinations can you make?
- Which sandwich would you want to try?
- Make up your own crazy sandwich. Write down the recipe.
- Is there something weird you like to eat? Describe it in a poem or story.

Cloudy with a Chance of Gumball

- Can you make a connection to this poem?
- Make a list of all the things you dream about? Keep a dream journal.
- Highlight all the rhyming words.
- Illustrate a picture of the poem.
- Create a bookmark to go with this poem.

If you Give a Frog a Fly

- Can you make any connections to this poem?
- Put the things Frog will do in order.
- Illustrate a picture of this poem.
- Reread it with a friend.

Emma and Bill

- What causes Emma and Bill to want to leave?
- Go to the library and learn about baby bears.
- Can you make any connections to this poem?

Snowflakes

- How would you feel if everyone was watching you do something?
- What types of things do you like to do in the snow?
- Highlight all the rhyming words.

Red

- Create your own color poem.
- Take a survey to see what the most popular color is among your friends.

Friendship

- What kind of activities do you like to do with your friends?
- Create an acrostic poem about Friendship.
- What memories do you have with a special friend?
- Do you remember the first friend you ever met?
- Make a list of words that describe friendship.
- What do you think the most important quality of friendship is?

Mr. Monkey and There's a Giraffe on my Bus

- What is your favorite zoo animal?
- Write a descriptive paragraph about visiting a zoo.
- Write a poem about a zoo animal.
- Where would you travel to on a bus?

Have you Ever?

- What would you wish if you could have a secret wish?
- Who are some people you would like to meet? Why do you want to meet them?
- Write a story or poem about an animal that has human qualities.

Butterflies and Ladybug

- Learn about the life cycle of butterflies. Draw a diagram of the cycle.
- Where would you fly if you were a butterfly?
- Butterflies are symmetrical, the same on both sides. Find other things around your house or school that are symmetrical.
- Find out 5 interesting facts about lady bugs and butterflies.
- What kind of flowers do butterflies like?
- Design your own flower to attract butterflies.

On the Farm

- What is your favorite farm animal?
- Do you think you would like to live on a farm? Why or why not?
- Highlight all the words that rhyme in this poem.
- Make a list of all the words that rhyme with pig, chick, goat and snake. Create your own poem.

Blessings

- What things are you grateful for?
- Turn this poem into a reader's theater for you and your friends.
- Illustrate a picture to go along with this poem.

My Little Ant

- Would you let an ant crawl on you? Why or why not?
- Pretend you are an ant. Write about what happens in your day.

A Witch's Broom

- **Write a story about an adventure you would like to have.**
- **What is your favorite book? Write a commercial convincing people to read it.**
- **Why does Witch's have an apostrophe *s?*** Find out the rules of using apostrophes.
- What would you do if you found pirate gold?

Apple of my Eye and Crocodile Tears

- Who is the apple of your eye?
- Apple of my eye is an idiom. What other idioms do you know? Find out what they mean.
- What does it mean to have crocodile tears?
- Illustrate 10 idioms.

Doctor's Office

- Can you make any text to self connections?
- Create a brochure showing that going to the doctors is important for good health.
- What advice would you give to a friend that was nervous about going to the doctors?
- Write your doctor a thank you note for helping you staying healthy.

Missing

- Write a mystery story.
- Create a scavenger hunt for you and your friends to play.
- Highlight all the rhyming words in the poem.
- Reread the poem until you memorize it, pretend you are a news reporter giving the information live in front of a crowd.

Georgie Porgie

- Do you like to plant a garden?
- What would you do to create a crowd?

Tickled Pink and I'm in a Pickle

- Who are you always happy to see?
- Underline all the rhyming words in the poem.
- What does it mean to be in a pickle?
- Have you ever felt like you were in a pickle?

I'm not a Turkey

- Pretend you are a turkey around Thanksgiving time, what would you do to trick the farmer?

Tofurkey

- Tofurkey comes from the two words tofu and turkey. Combine a few words together to come up with your own silly words.

Pet Peeves

- Pet Peeves are something that annoys you. Make a list of your pet peeves.
- Underline all the rhyming words.

Purple Hippo

- Purple Hippo was created by looking at a Christmas ornament. Look at the things around you right now. Pick one thing and make a list of all the words that pop in your head about that object. Then try to make up a story or poem about it.
- Pretend you are going skiing with your friends. Tell about your adventures.

Wolf's Story

- Can you make a text to text connection?
- Write your own version of The Three Little Pigs.
- Illustrate a picture to go along with this poem.
- Write a critique about this poem.

Platypus Paints

- Do you enjoy painting?
- Do you have a text to text connection?
- What is your favorite color?
- Make a book teaching children how to mix colors.
- Illustrate a picture to go along with this poem.

Doo-Doo MaGoo! And I Blew a Bubble

- Have you ever felt embarrassed? What did you do to make yourself feel better?
- Have a contest to see who can blow the biggest bubble, either with gum or bubbles.

Other things to do with poetry

- *__Parts of Speech Center__*--Color code parts of speech, and place on magnets. Each person using the center gets a package of color coded parts of speech, and must create sentences from them, posting the sentences on magnetic surfaces.

- *__Illustration Center__*--Have a collection of small poems copied. Have students divide up sentences, and make picture books of poem. Students could make picture books of their own poems. Students can also create a storyboard of their favorite poem.

- *__Listening Center__*--Students can record their favorite poems. Other students can listen to them.

- *__Reading Center__*--Display baskets of favorite poems for the students to read. Students can practice fluency, finding main idea, details, cause and effect, fact and opinion, compare and contrast and so much more.

- *__Editorial Center__*--Display interesting, and funny news articles. Students write an editorial poem on an event of their choice.

- Letter/sound associations

- *__Writing Center__* Have students continue the poem or answer questions the poem asks.

- *__Performing Poetry Center__*- Encourage kids to perform with props and gestures. Students can perform as duets also.

- **Poem Analysis Activity**--Once the basic poetry elements are taught, give a poem to the whole class. Split class into these groups: metaphor simile group, beginning and ending group, rhyme group, repetition and pattern group, physical form group. Each group gets ten minutes to analyze the poem based on their topic, and report back. Students should then find their element in one of their own poems.

- *__Missing Words Activity__*--Take out the most "poetic" words of a poem, and leave blanks in their place. Students must fill in the blanks. Share their poems, and then share the original. Students can then do this to their own poems in groups, and have other group members brainstorm other picture words to use in the blanks of each student's poem.

Some questions to help students respond to poetry.

How does the poem make you feel?

What was the main idea of this poem?

What images do you see when you read this poem?

Other types of Poetry

Bio Poem

Line 1: First Name
Line 2: Four descriptive traits
Line 3: Sibling of...
Line 4: Lover of
Line 5: Who fears...
Line 6: Who needs...
Line 7: Who gives...
Line 8: Who would like to see...
Line 9: Resident of...
Line 10: Last Name

Example:

Evan
Smart, clever, funny, strong
Sibling of Calvin the "Calvinator",
Lover of peanut butter and jelly,
Fears large shadows on the wall,
Needs to run around,
Gives great snuggles and hugs,
Would like to see a chicken dance,
Resident of Cumberland, RI.

Cinquain

Line 1 - a one word title
Line 2 - a 2 word phrase that describes your title
or you can just use two words
Line 3 - a 3 word phrase that describes an action
relating to your title or just actions words
Line 4 - a 4 word phrase that describes a feeling
relating to your topic or just feeling words
Line 5 - one word that refers back to your title

Example:

Apple (1 word)
Sweet, red (2 words)
In a tree (3 words)
Apples are the best (4 words)
Fruit (1 word)

Diamond Poem

Line 1 - a one word noun
Line 2 - 2 adjectives that describe the noun
Line 3 - 3 verbs that the noun does
Line 4 - 4 things (nouns) that the top noun and the bottom noun has
Line 5 - 3 verbs that the bottom noun does
Line 6 - 2 adjectives that the describes the bottom noun
Line 7 - a one word noun that is opposite the top noun

Example:

Dog

Big, friendly

Playing, licking, barking

Eyes, tongue, fur, tail

Purring, meowing, sleeping

Silky, furry

cat

COLOR:

A poem about your favorite color. Another easy form is to use the 5 senses-looks like, sounds like, smells like, tastes like, feels like.

Color looks like _____
Color sounds like_____
Color smells like_____
Color tastes like_____
Color feels like_____

Find one in the book!

Here are some even more ideas!

❀ Have a poetry picnic

❀ Have a poetry parade

❀ Create a poetry calendar

❀ Create a Poetry Lane

❀ Host a Poetry Party

❀ Design a Poetry Poster

❀ Design a Poetry Collage

❀ Have Fun!

Notes

Notes

Notes